THREE IN ONE

THREE IN ONE
A Book About God

ISBN 0-687-00710-0

05 06 07 08 09 10 11 12 13—10 9 8 7 6 5 4 3 2
PRINTED IN CHINA

THREE IN ONE
A Book About God

Lynne M. Lepley

Illustrated by

Florence Davis

Abingdon Press
Nashville

Dedicated to the glory of God and to all who
diligently seek to enter into the life of the Trinity.

Lynne Lepley

and to

Jack, John, and Will

Florence Davis

What is a tree?

It is more than just bark and branches.

A tree is roots—growing deep under the ground—reaching out to bring water and food to all the other parts of the tree.

No one sees the tree's roots, but everyone knows that they are there, because the tree is healthy and strong and alive. Without the roots, the tree would die.

tree roots
in the
ground

What is a tree?

It is more than just roots and bark and branches.

A tree is the fruit that starts as a tiny blossom.

The roots bring it food and water and it grows—
into fruit that is full and sweet and juicy.

ripe apricot
ready for
picking

We can take the tree's nourishment into ourselves whenever we eat the fruit part of the tree.

The seeds in the fruit are full of the roots' nourishment, too. They will die in the ground—but from the dying seed—a new tree will be born.

apricot seed

baked fruit pies
recipe found on last page

dried apricots

What is a tree?

It is more than roots and fruit and bark and branches.

A tree is the countless leaves that come to life in the wind.

They shimmer with the light of the sun in the summer—and set the tree afire with color in the fall.

What is a tree?

A tree is roots and fruit and leaves. They all look very different—and yet they are all the tree.

fruit

leaves

roots

Who is God?

God is the Father whom no one has seen.
But we know that God is there because we
have life and joy and blessing. We are alive.
We would die without God.

Who is God?

God is the Son. He is Jesus who was born a tiny baby that first Christmas in Bethlehem.

In the Father's care he grew strong and wise. He taught us about the Father.

He died on the cross and was buried—

but he rose to new life so we could come to new life too.

In Jesus we find sweet, refreshing spiritual food that comes from the Father.

apricot
blossom

Who is God?

God is the Holy Spirit (or Holy Ghost). The Holy Spirit is God's Spirit present with us.

The Holy Spirit is present in many places at one time. The Holy Spirit is the power and life of God within the hearts of those who love God.

The Holy Spirit was revealed to people in the Bible—sometimes as the breath of the wind—and other times as flames of fire.

We feel God's Spirit in our hearts.
Sometimes the Holy Spirit is like the cool,
refreshing wind.

Sometimes the Holy Spirit is like a fire,
burning warm within us.

Who is God?

Father, Son, and Holy Spirit. They all make themselves known to us in very different ways—and yet they are all God.

Praise God from whom all blessings flow;

Praise God all creatures here below;

Alleluia! Alleluia!

Praise God, the source of all our gifts!

Praise Jesus Christ, whose power uplifts!

Praise the Spirit, Holy Spirit!

Alleluia! Alleluia! Alleluia!

Baked Fruit Pies

Pastry
2 cups unsifted all-purpose flour
2/3 cup shortening
1 1/2 Tablespoons butter
1/3 cup plus 1 Tablespoon ice water

Filling
1 heaping cup dried apricots, chopped in small pieces
(dried peaches or apples may be substituted)
1 cup water
1/3 cup sugar
1 teaspoon butter

For pastry,
Cut shortening and butter into flour until crumbly. Lightly mix in water.
Roll into a ball and wrap in plastic wrap. Chill in refrigerator 1 hour.

For filling,
Cook dried fruit and a cup of water at medium low heat for about 15 minutes.
Reduce heat to low and stir in 1/3 cup sugar. Cook an additional 5 minutes or until slightly thickened.

Remove from heat and stir in 1 teaspoon of butter. Set aside to cool.

When pastry has chilled,
Break off a piece and roll out as thinly as possible. Place a 6-inch saucer on rolled dough and cut around to make a circle. Gather scraps of leftover dough and attach to remaining dough ball.

In center of dough circle, place 1 heaping Tablespoon of fruit mixture.
Fold one side over the fruit and press edges together with a fork. Cut 3 small slits in top of pie and place on baking sheet.

Repeat until all dough and fruit has been used. Recipe will make about 8 pies.

Bake at 325 degrees for about 40 minutes or until lightly browned.

Adult supervision is recommended.